DATE DUE			
AUG 1 6 1982			
AUG 3 0 1982			
JUL 1 0 1985			
APR 1 5 1986			
JUN 4 1986			
FEB 1 6 1987			
JUN 2 9 1988			
MAY 0 4 1998			

THE VOLLEY AND THE
HALF-VOLLEY

THE VOLLEY
AND THE
HALF-VOLLEY

The Attacking Game

by John F. Kenfield

UNITED STATES TENNIS ASSOCIATION
INSTRUCTIONAL SERIES

Illustrations by George Janes

DOUBLEDAY & COMPANY, INC.
GARDEN CITY, NEW YORK
1978

Library of Congress Catalog Card Number 76–56310
ISBN: 0-385-12633-6
Copyright © 1978 by John F. Kenfield
All Rights Reserved
Printed in the United States of America
First Edition

Library of Congress Cataloging in Publication Data

Kenfield, John F.
  The volley and the half-volley.

  (Instructional series)
  Bibliography: p. 61.
  1. Tennis—Volley. I. Title. II. Series.
GV1002.9.V65K46   796.34'22

Contents

THE VOLLEY AND THE
HALF-VOLLEY

I

The Theory of Net Play

This book is about that phase of tennis that is offense- or attack-oriented. When the player comes to the area of the court where the volley and half-volley are used, the intent is to win the point outright by one's own initiative. If this is not the case, the player has no business in the forecourt.

How well a player learns to volley, half-volley, and hit overheads depends upon several factors: natural skill, practice, and, most important, the attitude about how he or she wants to play tennis. A player who likes to make things happen rather than to wait for a mistake by the opponent has the right mental approach to become an attacking player. Those who like the security of the backcourt, have very good groundstrokes, and are patient may find it very difficult, purely from a psychological standpoint, to become a net rusher. At this point it is important to remind all erstwhile attackers that aggressive players do not abandon percentages and caution, but they are always looking for an opportunity to take the initiative and force the play. This, then, is the attitude that leads to good net play.

There are really only two important factors to be considered in order to understand the theory of net play: angle and time. To understand these principles, all you have to do is stand on a tennis court and visualize the possibilities. From a normal baseline position you will notice that it will be almost impossible to score a clear winner against your opponent unless you have your opponent far out of position and also hit the ball harder than safety dictates. The relatively narrow angles open to you definitely reduce your chances of achieving success with such strategy. Now, move up to the volleying position, let's say twelve to fifteen feet from the net. You will notice immediately that you now have much greater angles to place the ball away from your opponent. If the ball comes to you above net height and you move closer to the net, the angles and your consequent advantage get increasingly better. As a matter of fact, you don't have to go out on the court; here it is in a nutshell:

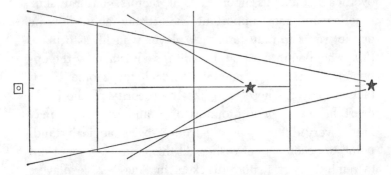

Recall that the other factor is time. When you are in the volleying position and play the ball from there, your opponent will have only a little more than half as much time to reach your shot as he or she would have had had you hit the ball from behind the baseline after it had bounced. We could employ all sorts of sophisticated electronic timing devices and give you the exact time advantages you steal from your opponent, but with or without technological data, the advantage is obvious.

There is one other angle advantage you gain when you are in the volleying position. For lack of a better term, let's call it the "safety" angle. When the ball comes to you above net height, you can hit as hard (within reason) as you want because you are hitting the ball *down* into the court. You don't have to lift it over the net and ease up to keep it inside your opponent's baseline. This principle is very important in doubles play because lateral angles are reduced. In singles, finesse and wide angles are what we want, and you should never hit the ball any harder than is necessary to win the point.

The Safety Angle

Superficially that's all there is to it. Playing the net makes a lot of sense, doesn't it? However, there is many a slip between theory and execution, and perhaps your opponents will have some ideas of their own. Some may be better at this strategy than you are. Perhaps they won't (certainly not willingly) put the ball right on your racket for a nice high forehand volley when you come in. The theory easily backfires unless the potential net player does a whole lot of things right. Doing them correctly and foiling the counterpunches of your opponent are what make the attacking game fun and exciting.

II

How to Get There

(Volleying Position)

Some of the ideas presented in this chapter are nuances of the game that concern only highly skilled players. However, they are important, and understanding them will add to one's enjoyment and understanding of the game as a spectator at matches. With this knowledge you can second-guess all the pro stars. And, of course, as you increase your own skills, more and more of these suggestions will be incorporated into your own game.

What the player does to arrive at the volleying position is the key to good net play. The volley, half-volley, and overhead, which will be dealt with in depth in succeeding chapters, are merely the weapons for administering the *coup de grâce*. The shot you hit to come in on is crucial. You may be the world's best volleyer, but you cannot make the time-and-angle theory work if your opponent zips the ball past you. Very simply, your approach shot to the net position should be good enough to force your opponent to make a weak return. What are these shots? How do you hit them? Where do you hit them?

TYPES OF SERVE

If you have a good serve it will provide an entree to the net. When following your serve to the net, it is essential to get your first serve in. From a psychological standpoint, the receiver feels much more pressure to make a good return when playing the first serve than when faced with a second serve. On your second serve the receiver is relaxed and is usually able to make a better shot. If you have a variety of serves (flat, slice, twist) you should mix them up, thereby keeping your opponent off balance and guessing. However, if a particular type of serve gives your opponent a lot of trouble, keep using it until he begins to make good returns consistently. It is not necessary to always use your "bullet" on the first serve. The very fast serve allows less time for the server to close on the net, and chances of getting it in consistently are reduced. Spin serves allow more margin for error and give the server an extra step toward the net, but they must land deep in the service court and be well placed.

TYPE OF SERVE AND PLACEMENT

When you discover a weak side in your opponent, most serves should go there. Otherwise, make use of percentage placement. From the deuce (right-hand) side, most serves that you intend to follow to the net should be placed in the center corner of your opponent's service court, as shown in the diagram. From the ad (left-hand) side, they should go to the outside corner. Your line of approach to the volleying position is also indicated in each diagram.

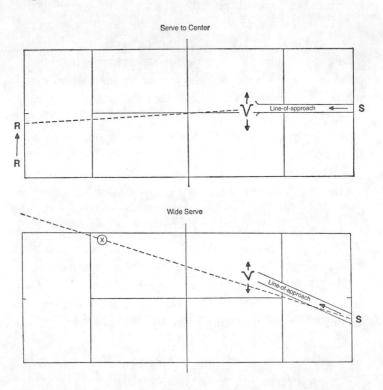

The above represent the best-percentage placements and are based on right-handed opponents with good forehands. If the reverse is true (either a left-hander or a weaker forehand), then you will adjust your percentage placements accordingly. If you have a good slice serve, perhaps every third or fourth attempt should be a wide slice to the opposite corner of your opponent's service court.

Serving directly at (jamming) your opponent is a very good idea. If the serve has good pace, it is very difficult for the receiver to move to the side of the oncoming ball quickly enough to make an accurate return. As a matter of fact, you will find that some players make excellent returns off your best wide serves. If so, try jamming them. Obviously there are a number of serves and placements at your disposal. Test your opponent, give him or her a lot of what they don't like, but also mix 'em up.

Service strategy in doubles is essentially the same except that, as the server, you must stand a little wider (to cover the alley) to begin your serve. Also, keep in mind that you are always trying to serve in such a way and place as to force the receiver to make a return that your partner at the net can reach and put away.

The position that your opponent takes to receive your serve will also have a bearing on the type and placement of serve you use. When the opponent stands in close (inside the baseline), a power serve is usually most effective; whereas if you find the opponent backing up to allow more time for handling your power, a serve with heavy topspin is usually effective in that it comes to the receiver at shoulder height and, because of the slower pace, it allows the server time to move in very close to the net before having to make the first volley.

MECHANICS OF FOLLOWING THE SERVE IN

It is also important to understand the mechanics of following the serve to the net—that is, angle of approach, footwork, balance, and body position.

First, you must toss the ball for your serve slightly more

forward (toward the net) than you do when staying back. This will give you more "lean" toward the net and will also force you to swing your rear foot through quickly as the initial step in your approach to the volleying position.

The next part of the approach is a controlled run; you want speed but not too much forward momentum, because you must come to a stop just before your opponent makes his shot. Most good players take four long running steps, the final step actually being a controlled forward jump onto both feet. The most common term for this jump is "split stop," and it leaves the player in a low (knees bent) position, facing the net, and ready to deal with any ball the receiver sends over the net. The number of steps may vary, as may the distance covered, but generally the player should be able to reach a spot just inside the service line. When the spin serve is used, an extra step may be possible, and the server may gain an extra yard or so toward the net.

Actually, you can get even closer to the net if you run as hard as you can and keep going, even as your opponent is hitting the ball. The trouble with this strategy is that it simply is not possible to move in two directions at the same time. Your opponent certainly will not hit the ball right at you (intentionally, at least). He will try to pass you, or perhaps lob you. Thus, charging in like a wild bull will put you at a very serious disadvantage. So the way to approach the net is with good, controlled hustle. If you are slow or lazy and do not get inside the service line, you will find yourself playing a lot of difficult shots from a very tenuous position. Get in quickly, but under control, and do a split stop just before your opponent hits the ball. Then you are ready for anything.

The line of your approach to the volleying position will depend upon the placement of your serve. Generally speaking, this line should bisect (divide evenly) the area of your own court that is open to the receiver's return. When you serve wide, your line of approach is to that side of the court, whereas a serve down the middle means your approach will be straight through the center of the court. When you serve extremely wide, you must approach the net at an angle that gives more than half of your coverage to the wide side. This is due to the fact that the down-the-line return is easier for the receiver, because there is very little margin for error on a crosscourt return. At any rate, when you serve wide, be especially alert for the down-the-line return.

These instructions may be rather difficult for some readers to follow and at the same time understand the logic of the suggestions. Here are diagrams that may help clarify the instructions.

Serve to Middle from Right Side
(shaded area shows receiver's possible angle of return)

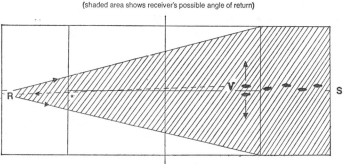

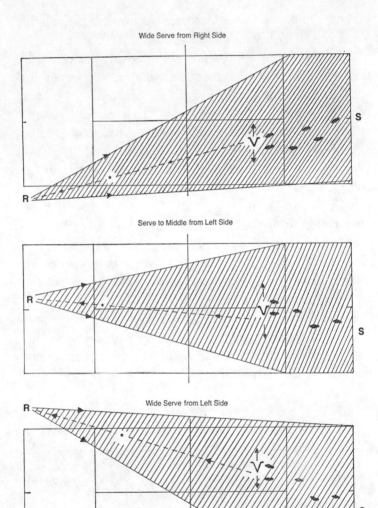

Wide Serve from Right Side

Serve to Middle from Left Side

Wide Serve from Left Side

The line of approach for doubles is essentially the same. The server takes his stance farther from the center of court in order to cover the alley, of course, but otherwise the strategy is the same. If your netman is a good volleyer and is aggressive, you can pretty much leave the center of the court up to your partner. If not, you must expect to take more shots in that area.

OTHER OPPORTUNITIES

There are, of course, many other occasions for players to go to the volleying position. A successful approach is most likely when two things occur: First, you get a *short* easy ball from your opponent, which is your opportunity; and second, you hit a *deep* forcing shot that he will have to hit from well behind his baseline. The short ball is important because it means that you will be hitting your approach shot from *inside* your own baseline, thus allowing plenty of time to move in close to the net. The depth of your own shot is important because it keeps the opponent back on defense and also allows you the extra fraction of a second you may need to reach his passing attempt. To be more specific, *any short ball*, unless the angle is such that you will be left far out of position and off balance, should be an opportunity for you to approach the net. Given this opportunity, what you then do with the ball will determine the success of your advance to the net.

PLACEMENT AND SPEED

The first rule to remember is not to overplay the ball. Many players in their eagerness to put pressure on the opponent will hit the forcing shot too hard and make many errors either by netting the ball or by driving it over the baseline. In other words, don't try to win the point with the approach shot. Win it the easy way by using your volley or overhead. Low balls especially must be played with a certain amount of caution because you must get the ball up and over the net and still keep it inside your opponent's baseline. High balls can be hit harder, because now you have the safety angle operating in your favor—you are able to hit the ball *down* into the court. In my opinion, most low approach shots should be topspin drives, and I favor the chop or slice on high balls.

Remember that any approach shot must land *deep* (preferably within a yard of the baseline) in the opponent's court, and it should have good pace. You should hit your forcing shots as hard as possible but still retain control of the shot. Remember that depth is the key ingredient. Extra speed on the ball won't help you much if your shot lands short.

Placement of the approach shot is important too. Short balls coming to you in the center of your half court may be hit to either corner, or even down the middle. However, by hitting to the corners you open more court for your winning volley. When the approach opportunity comes to you in the right or left one third of your court, your shot should almost always be down the line (to your opponent's corner on the same side). If you go crosscourt, you will leave a big opening for your opponent to pass you. You should hit crosscourt only when you have a clear opportunity for an easy winner on the shot you are hitting. When in doubt, go down the line. The reasoning behind these suggestions is shown clearly in the diagrams.

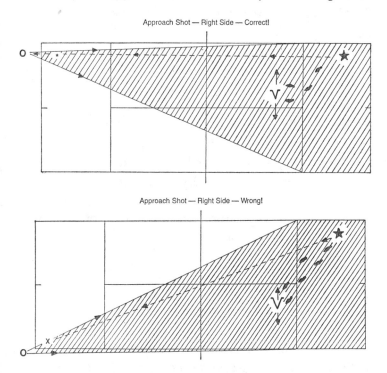

Approach Shot — Right Side — Correct!

Approach Shot — Right Side — Wrong!

The line of approach, footwork, balance, and so on are exactly the same as explained for following the serve to the net. The only real difference is that in many cases you will want to hit your approach shot "on the run." This takes good footwork and balance. However, when you have a little time bonus working for you, stop to hit the shot, which assures good balance, and then go in.

There are a few other occasions when the good player will take the net. If you return serve well, or if your opponent's serve is weak (a short shot!), you may come in behind your return. Net play is the name of the game in doubles, and the receiver must follow his return to the net.

Whenever you lob over your opponent and you realize he will have to scramble back to play the ball after it has bounced, you should hustle to the net in readiness for what you hope will be a weak return.

Occasionally when you get into a protracted baseline rally of soft deep shots with your opponent, you can be sneaky. What you do here is hit a nice deep sort of top-spin half-lob and then run very quietly to the net. If the opponent isn't paying strict attention, you are very likely to be given an easy setup since your opponent believes you to be a nice person who will stay harmlessly at the baseline.

OPPORTUNISTIC VOLLEYING

Another approach to the net requires alertness and the anticipation that comes with experience. Although a weak popup from your opponent could happen at various stages of a point, it is learning to anticipate the times when it is *likely* to happen that is important. Here is the situation: You have just hit a very sharply angled crosscourt shot that your opponent is tearing to reach before it bounces a second time in his alley. You sense that whether the opponent gets it or not is going to be very close but, in any case, even if successful, the return will be very weak, and your foe will be off balance and far over to one side. In this situation you can do one of two things: First, you can stand there on your own baseline admiring your great shot, laughing at your opponent's grunting effort and, of course, hoping the ball bounces twice. You are then amazed when the ball comes floating back to land directly in front of you. However, while you have been relaxing, the opponent has recovered and is camped securely in a strong volleying position in the center of his court. Had you been alert you could have taken advantage of your good angled shot. The moment you perceived that the opponent was in serious trouble, you should have taken a couple of steps inside your own baseline. Then, when the ball is popped up, you simply move forward and hit a soft, easy volley to the center of your opponent's court before he can recover. This is opportunistic tennis, and it pays off.

SOME WORDS OF CAUTION

This, then, is the how, why, and when of getting to the volleying position. Before going on to the mechanics of the volley, half-volley, and overhead, it may be well to throw in a few cautions or don'ts.

When you move up to the net, take care not to get too close. How close is too close? Well, you certainly don't want to hang your head over the net, for if your opponent has any brains at all, he will lob over you with ease. As mentioned earlier, the attacking player usually tries to play the first volley just inside his own service line. After making this shot he takes a couple more steps forward to reach the position he wants, which is one half to two thirds of the way back from the net and in front of the service line. He will move in closer when he sees an easy shot coming to him, but ordinarily never closer than the halfway point, because he must protect himself against the lob.

The neophyte net rusher must also take factors such as court surface, wind, sun, and background into account. The faster (that is, the smoother the finish) the court surface, the easier it is to make the volleying game effective. Although all hard courts (concrete, asphalt) are not finished with a smooth surface, in general they tend to be fast; whereas clay and composition are considered slow. The reason fast courts favor attacking players is that the ball, if hit with any authority, skids and picks up speed as it bounces, thus making forcing shots from the attacker more difficult to handle. Clay courts, or any court with a gritty surface, slows the ball down, and the ball bounces higher. These factors make all but the best forcing shots easy to deal with, and the advantage often lies with the defensive type of player. Also, clay and composition courts hold moisture, which gradually gets into the ball covering, making it heavier and slower. The grit surface also fluffs the cover of the ball, which further slows it down.

The reason for going into all these rather technical considerations is that they definitely do have a bearing on strategy. A player who likes to attack must learn to be more patient when playing on a slow surface. For instance, if you find that your serve seems to have lost all its effectiveness, perhaps you had best stay back after serving and wait for a short ball as your entree to the net. Your approach shots, which may have been very effective against the same or a similar opponent on fast courts, seem to be just the right speed and depth for your opponent to pass you on clay. All this might seem to indicate that you must change your own basic game or style of play when playing on different surfaces. Actually, this would be a very nice answer to the problem, but on the whole, most players have a particular method or style of play that suits them best, and when they attempt a different style they are not very good at it. The attacking, aggressive player should play his own game regardless of the surface. However, the really good ones will recognize the problems they face on slow courts and therefore learn to wait for exactly the right opportunity to come to the net. Their forcing shots and subsequent volleys will have to carry a little more zip, depth, and angle. The impatient net rusher is doomed on a slow surface.

A tailwind (behind you) favors the attacking player for the obvious reasons that it holds up and shortens your opponent's shots, while it adds depth and speed to your own. Again, though, the watchword is patience. Don't be in a tear to get to the net, because if you rush it you will make many needless errors. With the wind behind you, sooner or later your opponent will give you an easy opportunity to advance. Wait for it. Naturally, the same factor that is working for you with the wind at your back becomes a problem when you change sides. Try to be cagey by mixing up your serves and giving your opponent a lot of variety in the way of spins and angles. You will probably have to stay back and play defensively much more than you would like.

Crosswinds and gusts can be tough. You may mishit volleys and misjudge overheads and become very frustrated. There are a few suggestions that may help, the first of which is that you maintain your poise and concentration. Hit your approach shots and volleys to the side of court where the wind will carry the ball away from your opponent. However, do not try to sharpshoot. Allow more margin for error than usual.

Sun and background problems must be dealt with intelligently. For instance, if you like to follow your serve in but are still semiblind from the sun as you attempt your first volley, you will either have to try tossing the ball in a different place, not go in behind your serve when faced with this problem, or pray for a cloud. Lobbing into the sun is a smart move by an opponent. Sometimes letting the ball bounce will solve this problem for you. Occasionally because of a light background or perhaps too much sky behind your opponent, you may have great difficulty in picking up (visually) the ball as it comes off your opponent's racket. When this is the case, you must either temper your aggressiveness and stay back more, or perhaps choose an area of the opponent's backcourt that has better background as a target for most of your approach shots.

Thus we see that there are quite a number of things to be considered by the erstwhile attacker before he ever attempts the winning volley. However, as stated in the beginning, the proper method of arrival at the volleying position is the important part. Now let us examine the weapons at your disposal and show you how to use them so that you don't undo all the nice work you've done getting there.

III

Now That You Are There:

The Volley

It may be well to begin this chapter by trying to allay the fears of those readers who are actually afraid of playing the net. This fear is usually brought on by being forced to play the net before ready. It's much like the very real fear of water that people have who were either thrown in or perhaps fell in over their heads before learning to swim. Teaching these people to overcome their fear of the water is very difficult. Similarly, if a beginner gets into a doubles game (usually mixed, against an aggressive male opponent) and is told that he or she *must* play net and guard the alley—watch out! The competitive opponent, knowing the situation, will immediately try to intimidate the neophyte net player by hitting blasts either at the netman or down the alley. Two things could happen, either of which could be disastrous to the psyche of the person and to his or her future enjoyment of the game. To be hit by a hard-driven ball is not funny, but even if the person is agile enough to dodge, the blow to one's pride and consequent embarrassment will often be sufficient to cancel the desire to play the net. At any rate, the best advice here is to avoid situations like the above until you have learned to volley. Even if you have been "thrown in over your head," it is still possible to play the net and to enjoy it. Get a good teacher, practice a lot, and stay in your own league for a while. When you have learned to volley and are comfortable at the net, nothing is more fun.

THE GRIP

Grips for the various shots in tennis are always a subject for debate among the experts. As a matter of fact, you can learn to hit or volley *any* shot with almost *any* grip, providing you are not trying to hit the ball with the edge of the racket rather than the strings. However, the way you grip the racket determines the manner in which the racket is brought forward to meet the ball. Thus, the factors that lead to the determination of the "correct" grips are the limitations of the human anatomy and the tool (racket) you are using. The consensus seems to be that the Continental grip is the most adaptable for the various phases of net play.

If you will study the illustration, you will notice that this grip is about halfway between the Eastern forehand and the Eastern backhand grip. The apex (point) of the "V" between thumb and index finger is centered on the first level (flat surface) to the side of the top bevel of the handle as you hold the racket on edge.

The advantage of this grip is that it is a "universal" grip —that is, you can hit all the shots with it. Many players do use it for everything. The greatest advantage it has for volleying is that it is a time-saver. In quick exchanges at

The Continental Grip

the net, which occur frequently in doubles play, changing one's grip is almost an impossibility. Actually, rather minute but significant changes in this (Continental) grip are effected by shifting the heel of the hand at the butt of the racket in order to better accommodate switches from forehand to backhand and vice versa. Another advantage is that the Continental is the grip most players use for the serve. Thus the player does not have to change his grip when following the serve to the net.

The only real weakness of the grip shows up when one must volley very high balls—shoulder height or higher. In this case the Continental grip forces the player to make an exaggerated shoulder pivot and pronation (outward rotation) of the wrist on high backhand volleys, and an excessive supination (inward rotation) when playing high forehand volleys. Also, on high forehands the ball must be contacted much later than would be the case were the player using an Eastern grip.

The Eastern grip is advantageous in executing these high volleys. It gives the player "more thumb" behind the handle of the racket on high backhands, and the shoulder rotation need not be quite so severe. Therefore, players would do well to shift to the Eastern forehand and backhand grips when playing high balls. Certainly one can learn to do so when presented with a nice, easy put-away opportunity. Fast-moving high balls are another story, and you will have to stick with the Continental.

READY POSITION AND FOOTWORK

When in the volleying position, the ready position or stance is very similar to that of the backcourt. Feet should be comfortably spread, knees bent slightly, weight forward on the balls of the feet, and the racket held out front at about waist level. If there is a difference, it would be that the player should be slightly more crouched than when playing at the baseline. The reason for staying down (crouching) is twofold: First, remember that most shots from your opponent will be aimed to come to you as low as possible; second, there is a tendency to drop the head of the racket for low volleys when the player is too upright. It's easy to straighten up for high balls, but bend-

ing down for low shots seems to be difficult. So why not start in the best position?

The footwork used in making volleys is also much like that of the groundstrokes, except that when at the net one often lacks time to pivot properly and move into perfect position. Many balls will be played while facing the net and by stepping over to the ball with the near foot, rather than pivoting and stepping across. However, if the ball coming to you is slow enough, or if you need to move more laterally than a wide step will allow you, you should *always* pivot and step across.

When forced to go back to smash an opponent's lob, the first step should be a backward one with the foot on the side on which you intend to hit the ball. You continue with a series of sliding steps as far as you need to go before shifting the weight forward with a scissors kick to hit the overhead. Of course, if you are clearly lobbed over, you must turn your back to the net and scamper back to retrieve.

THE BACKHAND SYNDROME

The backhand syndrome is a desirable one. The accompanying illustrations prove the point. Whenever one is in the volleying position, especially when playing doubles, you should be mentally more prepared to play backhand than a forehand. Almost any ball coming to you within a foot or less of the *forehand* side of your body should be played with the backhand. The reason is purely anatomical. To prove this theory to yourself, take your racket and pretend that you must play a ball coming right at your navel. To do so with a forehand is impossible without moving your body to the side and out of the way of your elbow. Now try the backhand—it's easy! The only time this theory should be disregarded is when the ball is coming to you very slowly, you have time to move to the side, and you want to generate more power.

It is not possible to accurately judge how much greater a percentage of volleys will be played with the backhand, but it is considerable. The final factor to be kept in mind about developing the backhand syndrome is that while the player should be more ready for a backhand than a

forehand volley when engaged in rapid-fire volley exchanges at the net, one *should not* try to anticipate. This is one situation in tennis where anticipation can be disastrous. When you are expecting a forehand volley and the ball comes to your backhand, or vice versa, you will not be able to retract your incorrect assumption in time. Just be ready for anything, and watch the ball and your opponent's racket very closely. If he telegraphs his shot (does not conceal his intention), then anticipation is good. Just remember that the arc of coverage with the backhand volley is much greater than with the forehand volley.

THE HIGH FOREHAND VOLLEY

In discussing the mechanics of the volley there is a difference in the way the balls are played when coming above net height and below net height. For this reason, we will designate all balls coming to the player above net height as *high* volleys, and those arriving below net height as *low* volleys. Also, it may well be worthwhile to repeat the advice about always taking advantage of the safety angle discussed earlier—that is, whenever possible move forward (toward the net) to play the ball as high as possible rather than letting it drop below net height. High volleys are safer and may be hit harder.

When you watch an expert volleyer hit high volleys, whether they be forehand or backhand, it *appears* that there is more swing or stroking action in making these shots than there is when he is volleying low balls. This visual perception is true, but it is also deceptive. The

High Forehand Volley No. 1

High Forehand Volley No. 2

High Forehand Volley No. 3

High Forehand Volley No. 4

player does move his upper body more on high volleys, but there is very little, if any, more arm movement. The high volley does not require a bigger swing with the arm. If you will study the accompanying illustrations carefully, you will notice that the player rotates his upper body away from the oncoming ball and then rolls the shoulder on the hitting side into the shot. In other words, you get your racket back by turning your shoulder, rather than by drawing the arm back. Power is gained by the quickness with which the shoulder and arm are rotated forward to contact the ball, rather than by drawing the racket back with the arm and swinging it forward. You may also notice that the head of the racket is laid back slightly by cocking the wrist. This is to add power, but is usually not necessary, and beginning volleyers should forget it. Instead, try to keep a very firm wrist.

There is, of course, the standby adage of remembering to keep your eye on the ball, and when at the net this is frequently hard to remember, since there is an overwhelming urge to look at the spot in the opponent's court where you want your shot to go. Hit it, and then look!

When using the Continental grip, the ball is contacted about even with the player's head. Obviously, if one wants to go crosscourt, the ball is met "out front" a little more, and to go down the line requires more shoulder rotation and a later point of contact. If one uses an Eastern grip on these high volleys, then the point of contact is considerably farther forward, perhaps six to ten inches. As contact is made, the player continues to push or punch the racket head through the ball and simultaneously lets the face of the racket slide slightly under the ball. The spin achieved by going under the ball adds control and is slight enough not to sacrifice much power. At the end of the shot, racket head, arm, and shoulder are all pointing directly at the spot where the player wants the ball to go.

That's it, then, for the high forehand volley. The most apt description of the whole stroke is that it is a *punch* stroke that gets power from shoulder rotation and straightening the arm as the ball is hit. You needn't swing at the ball. Follow through, yes; but don't take a backswing.

THE HIGH BACKHAND VOLLEY

This stroke is almost identical to that used on the forehand side. The two main differences are that the shoulders must be rotated more radically, and, as in any backhand shot, the ball is met farther out front. The player in these illustrations is volleying down the line. You will notice that just prior to contact, the back is almost turned to the ball. Also notice that the shoulders do not rotate nearly so much on the follow-through as was true of the forehand. If the player wanted to go crosscourt, there would be more shoulder rotation in the follow-through.

All other facets of the high backhand volley are exactly the same as explained for the forehand. Generally, these volleys present an opportunity to win the point outright, or certainly allow the player to maintain an offensive advantage. Whenever possible, the ball should be angled strongly to whichever side of your opponent's court is open. Hitting the volley "behind" the opponent as he or

High Backhand Volley No. 1

High Backhand Volley No. 2

High Backhand Volley No. 3

High Backhand Volley No. 4

she is scrambling back to the center is a good idea occasionally, but don't overwork it.

Because there is practically no difference in the manner in which both forehand and backhand low volleys are made, we may discuss them simultaneously. They are played on opposite sides of the body, of course, and one uses a different face of the racket, but the stroke or *block,* as it might be termed, is essentially the same.

Because the opponent's shot is now coming to the player *below* net height, the "safety angle" advantage is lost. One must play these low balls a little more cautiously because of reduced angles and also because the ball must be hit *up* and over the net and still be kept within the opponent's baseline. As a matter of fact, unless your opponent attempts to lob over you, he or she will try to keep passing attempts as low and as wide as possible, thereby *not* giving you a chance to put the ball away. To counter these low and wide shots from your opponent you will often be forced to volley defensively. A good example is a ball that you have to stretch far to the side to reach and that you must play at ankle height. Some of the experts can turn these difficult shots into a winner for themselves by making a sharply angled stop volley, but it is not a shot that carries much percentage with it, and it requires great touch, which comes only with experience and long practice. However, all low volleys need not be defensive shots. You still have the time advantage, some angle advantage, and if your approach shot forced your opponent, you can score many winners, even from shoe-top level. When you can do these things you are ready for the circuit!

The first thing you should notice from the following illustration of a very low forehand volley is that the player has *really* lowered his body to make the shot. You must "get down with the ball" to consistently make good volleys at this height.

There is less shoulder rotation than we noted in discussing high volleys, but it is still there. However, the stroke is now more a simple reaching out to meet or block the ball with your racket. It doesn't really look much like a swing at all, and it isn't. The plane of the racket (lengthwise) is kept more or less parallel with the ground, and the racket face is angled just enough to get the ball over the net. One should always reach well out in front of the body to play these low volleys—much more so than when playing high shots. The stroke is merely a straightening of the arm to reach out and block the on-coming ball. Balls that are coming directly at the player are always played with the backhand, and there is no shoulder rotation whatsoever (see illustration). The ball is met with a flat (no underspin) racket for power, but if more control is desired, the player allows the face of the racket to slide slightly under the ball. You will also notice that the follow-through is much less pronounced than is evident on high volleys.

The key factors to remember when practicing low volleys are to start and stay low, watch the ball very closely, and reach out front to meet the ball. The last chapter will treat various exercises to practice all aspects of the net game.

Low Forehand Volley No. 1

Low Forehand Volley No. 2

Low Forehand Volley No. 3

Low Forehand Volley No. 4

Low Backhand Volley No. 1

Low Backhand Volley No. 2

Low Backhand Volley No. 3

Low Backhand Volley No. 4

DOUBLES DIFFERENCES

The final factor the reader should be apprised of is the difference in strategy between singles and doubles when playing low volleys. In singles your opponent is usually in the backcourt hoping you will popup an easy ball so that he or she can pass you. This means that whenever you are forced to volley defensively your shot should keep the opponent well behind the baseline. Angle it to force the opponent out of position as well, if you can, but most of all, *keep it deep.*

In doubles the situation is completely different. Now both opponents are at the net (volleying position), and if you attempt a deep volley it will also be high. This is exactly what they want, and they will ram the ball right down your throat. Now your strategy on low volleys is to keep the ball as close to the net and as low as possible, forcing them to hit up. Soft, low volleys are often the best in this situation. The first team that pops one up will have to eat it.

There is still another difference that is worth consideration here. In singles you almost always attempt to angle your shots away from your opponent. In doubles these angles are greatly reduced, because you face the lateral coverage of two opponents. For this reason most shots are aimed to go between your opponents. By so doing you hope to confuse them and cause them to let the ball go untouched between them. In other cases, you and your partner try to aim your shots directly at an opponent, preferably right at the feet. Playing a volley from there is very difficult, and even if the player is able to make a return, it is almost always so weak that it is a setup.

There are a couple of other rules for percentage volleying in doubles that are worth mentioning. "Closing" and "holding" are terms used to designate the players' position relative to the net. Whenever your team has just made an offensive shot—that is, low and difficult for your opponents to handle—both of you should move in a step or so closer to the net in anticipation of a weak return. When on offense, you *close* on the net. When your shot is weak or one that will merely maintain the status quo of the point, then you and your partner should *hold* your position. You retreat only when to do otherwise would be foolhardy. It is very difficult to teach players to close on the net. The problem is that by the time they realize they had a chance to move in, it is often too late to take advantage of the opportunity. One must really concentrate on anticipating the opportunity to close. It must become a conditioned reflex and is the mark of a knowledgeable and good doubles player.

The other percentage rule that good doubles players always follow is that whenever they are playing the ball offensively (usually from above net height), their shot is aimed to go at or through the opponent who is nearer. If playing a defensive (low) volley, the player tries to keep the ball to the side of the opponent who is farther from the net. The reason for this advice is simple. When on offense volleys may be hit harder and also on a downward angle. You aim these shots at the opponent who is closer to you because that opponent will have less time to react and make the return than will the one who is farther away. Conversely, when in trouble you want more time to recover and be ready for the opponents' next shot, so you hit to whichever of them is farther from the net. If both have closed, which they should do, your side is in deep trouble. When playing the ball offensively and you have one opponent at the net and the other back, *never* play the ball to the person in the backcourt. *Always* go between them or through the "up" man.

Finally, play the weaker opponent. Although both opponents may be excellent doubles players, one is usually a little quicker or perhaps more devastating in volley exchanges. Determine which of them is better, and keep the ball to the other side as much as possible.

SOME INNOVATIONS

Up to this point we have discussed only the "standard" volleys and, of course, they are the ones that must be mastered before a player attempts more exotic ways of playing the ball when at the net. However, as one's skill, confidence, and touch progress, the stop-volley and the lob-volley will become part of your repertoire.

The stop-volley is nothing more than a drop shot made from a volley. Generally it is attempted on low volleys when the opponent is well back in the court and the player making the volley is unable to make a good enough standard volley to keep the opponent on defense. If the attempt is poor, your shot will give the opponent a setup; but if good, it will score many easy winners because the opponent will not have time to react quickly enough to get to the ball. Incidentally, the stop-volley is rarely used in doubles, because one or the other of your opponents will almost always be able to get to the ball.

In appearance the stop-volley closely resembles any other volley. The difference lies in the fact that the player does *not* hit the ball; instead, one sort of *lets* the ball hit the racket. There may even be a slight backward motion of the racket as ball meets strings in the effort to keep the ball from rebounding too much. In any case, the shot is usually angled sharply away from the opponent, just barely clears the net, and lands very short in the opponent's court. Backspin, which is one of the ingredients of a drop shot from the backcourt, is not particularly necessary when making a stop-volley, but turning the face of the racket under the ball as it contacts the strings will help make the resulting bounce in the opponent's court shorter. This is a very difficult shot to make from much above net height because the bounce in the opponent's court will be too high. It is a great shot, and when you can execute a perfect stop-volley, it will add a new dimension of fun to your game. But don't overdo it. Use it only when an easier way of winning the point is not possible.

The other innovation is the lob-volley. One sees this shot used mostly in doubles matches. The occasion to use it arises when one is caught in midcourt (at or near the service line) and both opponents are right on top of the net. In this situation the player realizes that any shot other than a lob over both opponents will spell disaster for his team, so he blocks the ball with a sharply angled racket face in an attempt to get it over them and force them back. If the attempt is a good one, the opponents will have to turn tail and scamper back to play the ball after it has bounced, thereby relinquishing the offense to the lobbing team. If really good, and your opponents are napping, it may even get you a winner. If not quite deep enough, the opponent will be able to hit an overhead, but perhaps you or your partner will be able to throw up another (hopefully better) lob. If it is too short or too low, your strategy will have come to naught. Because the lob-volley is a very satisfying ego pleaser when it works, many players tend to get carried away by their success and try to use it too much. One should still think of it as primarily a defensive shot and use it when nothing else will work. A good lob-volley requires great touch, much as does the stop-volley, and remember: Use it sparingly. Otherwise, after a couple of attempts your opponents will begin to suspect your intention and will lay back in readiness to smash the ball.

So now you know all about volleying. There are, however, a couple of other shots you may have to play when you come to the net. Let's look at them and find out how to handle these other situations.

IV

When You Can't Volley:

The Half-Volley and the Overhead

Your opponent will do everything in his power to keep
you from volleying. You will be passed whenever possible, but let's concern ourselves in this chapter with the
shots you are able to reach but are unable to volley.

THE HALF-VOLLEY

You will recall that whenever your opponent is unable
to get the ball by you, his or her shots will be aimed to
come to you as low and as wide as possible, unless, of
course, the ball is lobbed over your head. Passing attempts
almost always have these two features: low over the net
and as wide as possible. You will sometimes have to handle
these shots even though your approach shot is above re-
proach. Some of these shots are going to dip so low over
the net that they will bounce before you can reach them,
and when that happens you must play a half-volley.

Before going into the mechanics of this shot, it may be
well to offer a few more strategic suggestions. First, when
you see one of these shots coming, reach forward to volley
it before it strikes the ground, when you can. This oppor-

Half-Volley No. 1

Half-Volley No. 2

Half-Volley No. 3

Half-Volley No. 4

tunity arises occasionally when the opposing player hits a soft shot that will land right at your feet if you remain stationary but that, if you are alert and ready, you can move forward a step or two and play more aggressively by volleying the ball. This amounts to one of the cardinal principles of net play: Never use a half-volley when you can volley instead! There is, however, one instance when this rule is violated: If the shot coming to you is very slow, has backspin, and will bounce nice and high after hitting the court, let it bounce and rise, thereby affording a chance to hit down on the ball and put it away. Actually, of course, your shot is not a half-volley at all, but the situation is such that you could have played a half-volley.

The term "half-volley" is used to describe shots that are played *immediately* after the ball bounces. When a player allows a ball to rise more than six to eight inches, he is playing the ball "on the rise," but he is not hitting a half-volley. Therefore, one of the secrets of making a good half-volley is to play it just after it comes off the bounce. Don't let it rise.

The Continental grip, which was advocated for the volley, also serves very well for half-volleys; also, because the shot is played in exactly the same manner, whether the shot is a forehand or a backhand, one description will do for both sides. One does almost exactly the same things required to make a low volley—watch the ball very closely, lower your body, keep the racket head up, and don't hit very hard.

Again, as in making low volleys, there is little or no backswing. One simply reaches out to put the face of the racket directly behind the spot where the ball will bounce. The angle of the face of the racket is almost perpendicular to the ground but will vary slightly depending upon what the player intends to do with the ball. At this point in the execution of the shot, things get different. Now, instead of allowing the racket face to slide *under* at contact, the ball is more or less smothered with topspin; the racket face is lifted up and over the ball with a rolling action. It is a rather wristy stroke, and the ball is sort of flipped over the net. The follow-through is short but fairly high. You will notice from the illustrations above that, as in low volleys, the ball is met well out in front. The main thing to remember is that you want topspin. The shot can be made with backspin, but is less accurate, and the backspin causes the ball to "sit up" for the opponent after the bounce.

Because the player is close to the net and is playing the ball from shoetop level, most half-volleys are categorized as defensive shots. From this position one cannot hit the ball with any authority, have it go over the net, and still stay in the court; hence the topspin is added. This spin, which will help bring the ball down into the court after passing over the net, allows the player to hit the shot a little harder than would be possible without topspin. The spin also allows a greater margin for error as the ball passes over the net.

Since the half-volley is primarily a defensive shot, the strategy is the same as when playing a low and difficult volley. One should try to maintain parity by keeping the ball deep in the opponent's court. If one can force the opponent out of position or achieve an angle that will win the point, so much the better, but think primarily of playing the shot deep enough to keep your opponent in a defensive situation. Of course, the topspin and soft, short stroke are the keys to realizing this objective. You can't hit it hard because the ball is so low, so you play it soft and deep.

The half-volley is a shot you will have to play frequently in doubles when you follow your serve to the net. The strategy when playing half-volleys in doubles is to keep the ball very low and close to the net. You must make the shot very soft so that it will drop very quickly after passing over the net. Anything that comes to your opponents above net height will be a put-away for them.

MORE GLAMOROUS SHOTS

Offensive shots that will often win the point can be made with the half-volley. The half-volley drop shot is the epitome of touch in tennis. To attempt this shot one must have the same strategic situation called for on stop-volleys: The opponent must be in the backcourt, and the player making the attempt must be in a rather desperate situation, feeling that almost any other shot would set the ball up for the opponent. Additionally, you must have confidence in your ability to "pull it off" a majority of the time. For a player with great touch it is not a desperation shot, but generally it is *not* a good percentage shot, for it is one of the most difficult shots in the game. Here is a case where a player not only bails out of a very tenuous position, but wins the point as well. Executed perfectly, it is a thing of beauty and very demoralizing to the opponent.

The real secret of the half-volley drop is touch or feel. As in the stop-volley, one simply lets the oncoming ball rebound against the strings. There is practically no follow through in the stroke, and one doesn't worry about spin. You just try to "dink" it over the net, generally on a sharp angle away from your opponent. Your success with the shot will be determined by how well you have judged the speed of your opponent's shot and by *how much* you let the ball *rebound* from your racket. If you stop it too much, the ball will go into the net; if you fail to stop it enough, the ball will either go out or give your opponent an easy shot to win the point. Remember: If your opponent is sharp, he or she will be looking for an opportunity to move forward to volley your return if you pop it up. Therefore, your shot must be so good as to be impossible for the opponent to reach.

Another exotic shot that is perhaps even more difficult to execute, and attempted when the situation is even more desperate, is the half-volley lob. A typical situation for attempting a lob off the half-volley is one where you are caught far out of position and your opponent hits a hard-driven ball (probably an overhead smash) just inside your baseline and you are barely able to reach it. All you can do is to make a stab at returning the ball. Your opponent, of course, is camped in a very commanding position at the net. Given this situation, you know that your only chance of getting back in the point is to throw up a good lob that forces the opponent back to hit another overhead. Here again, touch is of the essence. You do not have the time or balance to stroke a lob, so you simply trap the ball on the rise, flick the sharply angled racket head with your wrist, and hope that you have made a decent lob. This is definitely a "hit and hope" shot, but when nothing else is possible, you have no alternative. A player with great touch will get away with it occasionally.

The half-volley is an indispensable part of an attacking

player's repertoire. It is your defense against the best shots the opponent can mete out—except, of course, the passing shots you simply cannot touch. And, if you are a great half-volleyer, you can turn the tables on your opponent with cleverly executed touch shots. Practice suggestions for learning the half-volley are included in the final chapter.

THE OVERHEAD

Discussion of the overhead in this book will be very brief. The serve and the overhead are treated in depth in another United States Tennis Association series book by the same publisher. However, since the overhead is really a volley (hit in the air), at least a limited explanation is indicated here.

When one advances to the volleying position, one must expect the opponent to lob—sometimes occasionally, sometimes frequently. If your overhead is weak, you may see a lot of these sky balls. Also, if your opponent is cagey and disguises his shots well, he or she will give you a well-calculated mixture of passing attempts and lobs. In any case, the overhead smash is an integral part of the attacker's game.

Position and timing are the two chief ingredients of the overhead, and they come only with many hours of practice. The smash is often neglected by players who are not truly dedicated to learning all facets of the attacking game, because learning it and practicing it are probably the hardest work one has to do. Hitting fifty or one hundred in a row is exhausting, yet it is the only way to learn. Stay with it.

One final word of advice: When you find that you are not in a good position to hit an overhead, whether due to the wind blowing or to your own negligence, *do not* try to take a full swing and put the ball away. If you do, your chances of making the shot are far below a reasonable percentage. Instead, swallow your pride, even though you know you had an opportunity for a winner, and simply punch a deep volley into the corner of your opponent's court. This will keep the opponent on the defensive and, more important, you will avoid a needless error. Don't take a chance when you are out of position.

By now, if you have managed to stay with this book from the opening paragraph, you should have a very comprehensive picture and, hopefully, an understanding of the attacking game. The last chapter is a series of suggestions as to how to go about learning and practicing these various skills.

V

How to Practice and Learn

Most people begin learning tennis from the baseline. For this reason we are most comfortable on the court when hitting forehand and backhand ground strokes. Leaving this security and learning how to play the net can be a very frustrating and long process. Unless convinced that the ability to volley, half-volley, and hit overheads is important, many persons will give up, deciding that they will stick with the familiarity of the backcourt. Learning to play the net *is* frustrating, and in the early stages of the process one feels very insecure. Thus the first thing the erstwhile attacker must do is to develop an attitude of perseverance and a determination to learn.

You cannot learn to play the net from the baseline. In other words, you must go in and make attempts at rushing the net whenever the opportunity arises. You may feel that you have a much better chance of winning the point and possibly the match if you stay back, even when you are handed a perfect opportunity to advance. If this is the case, you are succumbing to the desire to win. That's O.K., but you will never learn to volley with this attitude. When learning you must take advantage of every opportunity, even though you feel that you will flub the chance a majority of the time. One doesn't become an effective attacker overnight. Many mistakes, losses, and subsequent frustrations must be "lived through" before one achieves competence. So with this "proper attitude" firmly in mind, let's discuss ways and means of becoming an attacking player.

VOLLEYING FOR BEGINNERS

Perhaps the place to begin is with an assessment of your physical limitations, whether your age is six or sixty. You will not be able to classify yourself as a complete net player if you haven't the strength, speed, and endurance to chase lobs that go over your head. These requirements alone are the deciding factors as to whether or not you can be a net rusher in singles. In doubles, however, all players must learn to play at the net if they are to make a contribution to their team.

Beginners should understand the theory of net play, know the correct grip, strokes, and so on, and then get either a colearner or a ball-throwing machine to practice against. In the early stages of learning, it is best to take shots on one side only, say the forehand, and later practice backhands only. This will allow you to concentrate on the mechanics of one shot alone without having to worry about where the ball is coming to you. When you feel that you can handle shots to either side pretty well, have your practice mate feed you alternate forehands and backhands. The final step, of course, is for the feeder to hit random shots.

The steps in this process should be slow, and the difficulty of the shots should be increased only as competence is gained. In the beginning the feeder should hit only nice, soft shots that come to the learner exactly where he or she is expecting the ball. Practice low ones and high ones, and then a variety on the same side. Also, when practicing backhand volleys, be sure to have the feeder hit a lot of balls right at you so that you can develop the backhand syndrome. Once you are able to handle a variety of random shots on both sides, you are ready to start practice exercises that resemble match conditions.

ADVANCED VOLLEYING PRACTICE

If you intend to use your newly learned skills for singles play, you will certainly want to include approach shots in your practice drills. Your first and most obvious approach is behind your serve. To begin with, you and your practice partner should agree that the receiver will make returns that the server can reach and volley. As the volleyer, go for a winner if you can, but certainly make that first volley deep. This exercise involves only three shots: the serve, the return, and the first volley. Try it ten times from alternate courts and then change jobs with your partner. When you are able to make seven or eight of ten good first volleys, the difficulty of the exercise should be increased. Now the receiver makes the returns of service as difficult as possible. The final step, of course, is to actually play points, still taking ten turns apiece, but do not keep score.

The next drill involves advancing to the net from the backcourt. You will notice from the diagram that three or four people can participate in this drill. As a matter of fact, having more than one person practicing approach shots is time-saving, because there is no wait while the person practicing the approach and volley goes to the backcourt after each attempt. Here is how it works:

Setup for Approach and Volley Drill

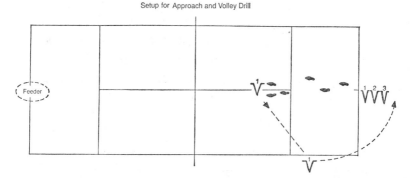

The feeder hits short balls (both high and low bounces) that the attacker plays as well and as forcefully as possible without actually attempting to win the point on the approach shot. The feeder then makes a return that gives the volleyer a chance to win the point. If the feeder misses the setup shot, he or she will immediately send up a lob with an extra ball, thus giving the advancing player an opportunity to hit an overhead smash. As the attacker, as soon as you have hit your shot you move to the side and back, allowing the feeder to hit to the next attacker in line. As with the previous exercise, difficulty should be increased as skill is gained so that eventually the points are played out. When only two players use this drill, it should be understood that after making the volley, the attacking player should turn immediately and run to the backcourt as though chasing a lob. Doing this will speed up the drill, and the player rushing the net will get a very strenuous workout. As a matter of fact, if you have plenty of balls, the feeder may send up a lob immediately after the net rusher hits his volley, even though it may have been a winner. As mentioned, this will increase the difficulty of the drill, create a matchlike situation, and will give the attacking player a very tough workout.

This sequence—approach shot, volley, and then either a lob or a continuation of the point—cannot be practiced too much. Vary it to work on your weaknesses—say, by having the feeder give you all low balls on your backhand for your approach, or have your practice partner return your first volley, which you have intentionally hit back down the middle, by throwing up a lob. Vary the drill intelligently so that both of you practice what you most need to practice. Although the ultimate objective of this exercise is to produce match conditions, do not keep score. Once you do so, the practice attitude will be lost, and you will start worrying more about winning the point than concentrating on what you are trying to learn. Incidentally, the feeder gets almost as much practice as the attacker by hitting controlled passing attempts and lobs.

QUICKNESS DRILLS

One of the best ways to improve your reflexes and agility is to stand twelve to fifteen feet from a backboard and practice volleying against yourself. Start by hitting fairly softly and high on the backboard. As you improve, move in a little closer and start hitting harder and lower.

Another good drill for developing quickness at the net is what might be called one-on-one, two-on-one, or two-on-two drills. In one-on-one, the two players stand opposite each other in the volleying position and rally with volleys and half-volleys. Do not try to hit the ball away from your practice partner; rather, try to keep the rally going as long as possible. To add fun and competition, play a game of twenty-one points, each player getting five serves before changing. There are only two rules: The ball must pass over the net three times before each point "counts," and points may not be won by hitting the ball away from your opponent. You must either hit it through him or make him miss. The three-hit rule is to prevent the "server" from gaining an advantage by starting the rally with a very difficult shot.

When three players (two-on-one) are involved, the rule is changed for the single player: He may win the point by hitting the ball anywhere within his opponents' court, while the doubles team must go through him or make him miss.

Two-on-two is a very real simulation of doubles play after the serve and return. The three-hit rule is retained in serving, but the point may be won in any manner. It is usually best to play this game using regulation point- and game-scoring and tie-breakers. This means that the partners always play on the side of the court that would be their normal position when receiving and, of course, they alternate right and left sides when serving. The beauty of this drill is that it is exactly like regular doubles, except that serve and return are eliminated. It develops quickness with the racket, and it is fun.

PRACTICING THE HALF-VOLLEY

Any time you practice volleying you will also have to make some half-volleys, and once you have learned the shot, this practice, which combines both shots, is probably good enough. However, how can you practice *only* half-volleys? As a matter of fact, this is almost impossible unless you can set up a ball-throwing machine that will consistently spew balls right at your feet. If you can find a really good practice partner (a pro?) to act as feeder, you will probably be able to get 50 per cent or more of the shots coming to you in such a way that you will be able to half-volley them. In order to make it a little easier for the feeder, it is best to have the person practicing half-volleys take up a position farther from the net than the normal (twelve to fifteen feet) volleying position—roughly on the back service line. By dropping back you make it easier for your practice partner to keep shots low so that they will bounce in front of you. Practicing the half-volley specifically is difficult indeed. However, advanced players rarely try to do this, because they will get plenty of practice from the random shots that come whenever one is at the net position. Learning this shot generally goes hand-in-hand with learning to volley.

There are, of course, many other drills and exercises that may help you learn the attacking game. Almost all of the books listed in the bibliography contain some ideas that may appeal to you. Also, it's fun to dream up and experiment with ideas of your own.

Good luck.

Bibliography

Addie, Pauline Betz. *Tennis for Everyone.* Washington, D.C., Acropolis Books, 1973.

Barnaby, John M. *Advantage Tennis.* Boston, Mass.: Allyn & Bacon, 1975.

Conroy, John. *The Tennis Workbook—Unit II.* Princeton, N.J.: USTA Publications, 1975.

Faulkner, Ed, and Weymuller, Fred. *Ed Faulkner's Tennis: How to Play It, How to Teach It.* New York: Dial Press, 1970.

———. *Ed Faulkner's Tennis* (pocket edition). New York: Dell Publishing Company, 1973.

Gould, Dick. *Tennis Anyone?* Palo Alto, Calif.: Mayfield Publishing Company, 1971.

Haynes, Connie, with Kraft, Eve, and Conroy, John. *Speed, Strength, and Stamina: Conditioning for Tennis.* Garden City, N.Y.: Doubleday & Company, 1975.

Hopman, Harry. *Better Tennis for Boys and Girls.* New York: Dodd, Mead, & Company, 1972.

Johnson, Joan, and Xanthos, Paul. *Tennis.* Dubuque, Ia.: William C. Brown Company, 1972.

Kenfield, John F. *Teaching and Coaching Tennis,* 3rd ed. Dubuque, Ia.: William C. Brown Company, 1976.

King, Billie Jean, with Chapin, Kim. *Tennis to Win.* New York: Harper & Row, 1970.

Kraft, Eve. *The Tennis Workbook—Unit I.* Englewood Cliffs, N.J.: Scholastic Coach Book Services, 1975.

Lardner, Rex. *Tactics in Women's Singles, Doubles, and Mixed Doubles.* Garden City, N.Y.: Doubleday & Company, 1975.

Laver, Rod, with Pollard, Jack. *How to Play Championship Tennis.* New York: The Macmillan Company, 1972.

Murphy, Bill, and Murphy, Chet. *Tennis for the Player,*

Teacher, and Coach. Philadelphia: W. B. Saunders Company, 1975.

Murphy, Chet. *Advanced Tennis.* Dubuque, Ia.: William C. Brown Company, 1970.

Schwed, Peter. *Sinister Tennis.* Garden City, N.Y.: Doubleday & Company, 1975.

Talbert, William F. *Sports Illustrated Book of Tennis.* Philadelphia: J. B. Lippincott Company, 1972.

Talbert, William F., and Old, Bruce S. *The Game of Singles in Tennis.* Philadelphia: J. B. Lippincott Company, 1962.

———. *The Game of Doubles in Tennis.* Philadelphia: J. B. Lippincott Company, 1962

Van der Meer, Dennis, and Olderman, Murray. *Tennis Clinic.* New York: Hawthorn Books, 1974.

With the co-operation of the United States Tennis Association, Doubleday has published the following titles in this series:

SPEED, STRENGTH, AND STAMINA: Conditioning for Tennis by Connie Haynes with Eve Kraft and John Conroy
Detailed descriptions of exercises for tennis players, and suggestions for keeping in shape.

TACTICS IN WOMEN'S SINGLES, DOUBLES, AND MIXED DOUBLES, by Rex Lardner
A book for women tennis players, with specific suggestions for taking advantage of opponents' weaknesses.

SINISTER TENNIS, by Peter Schwed
How to play against left-handers, and also with left-handers as doubles partners.

RETURNING THE SERVE INTELLIGENTLY, by Sterling Lord
How you can reduce errors, minimize the server's advantage, and launch your own attack.

COVERING THE COURT, by Edward T. Chase
How to be a winning court coverer and keep maximum pressure on your opponent.

THE SERVE AND THE OVERHEAD SMASH, by Peter Schwed
How the intermediate player can best hit the big shots.

FINDING AND EXPLOITING YOUR OPPONENT'S WEAKNESSES, by Rex Lardner

THE VOLLEY AND THE HALF-VOLLEY: The Attacking Game, by John F. Kenfield

TENNIS DRILLS FOR SELF-IMPROVEMENT, edited by Steven Kraft, USTA Education and Research Center
Ten of the nation's top young tennis coaches offer forty-two favorite drills.

The following titles are in preparation:
GROUND STROKES
THE TENNIS PLAYER'S DIET
SPECIALIZATION IN SINGLES, DOUBLES, AND MIXED DOUBLES